Quartette

Living through loss and learning through love;
poetry for the soul

Ashley Marie Godinho

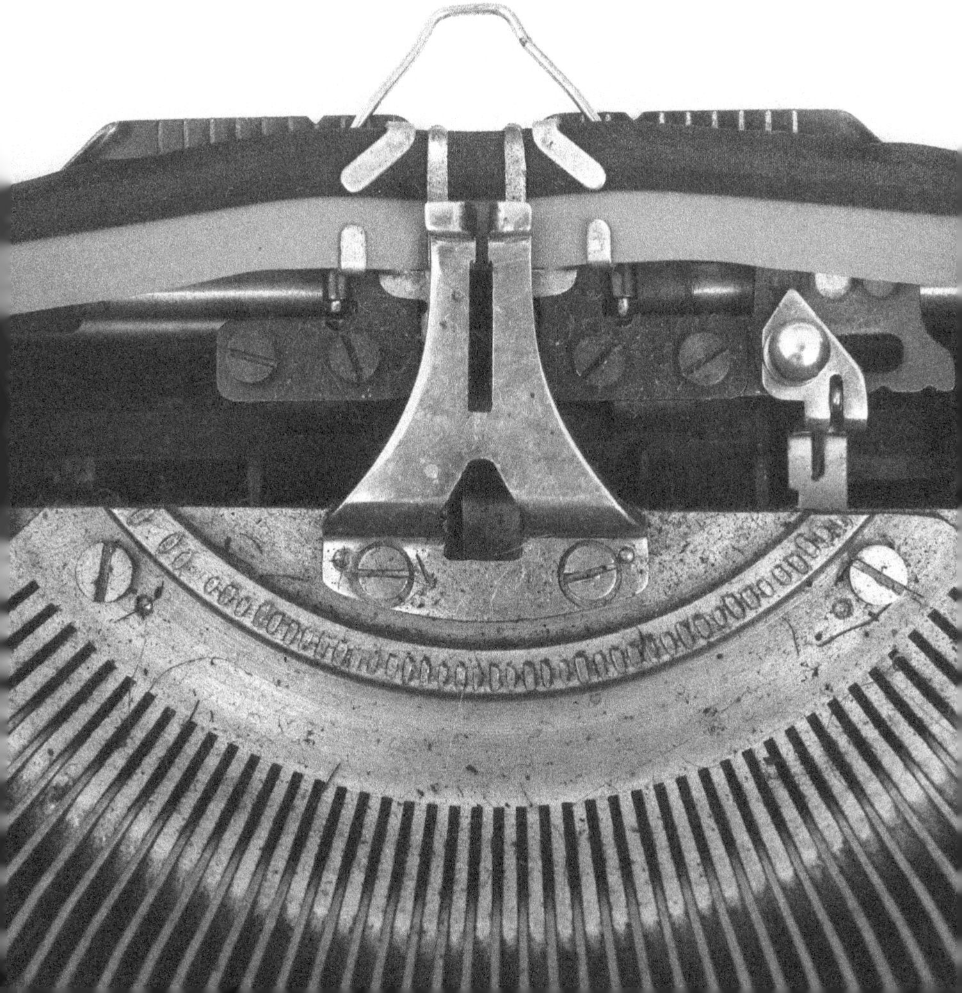

FriesenPress

Suite 300 - 990 Fort St
Victoria, BC, V8V 3K2
Canada

www.friesenpress.com

Copyright © 2021 by Ashley Marie Godinho
First Edition — 2021

All rights reserved.

No part of this publication may be reproduced in any form, or by any means, electronic or mechanical, including photocopying, recording, or any information browsing, storage, or retrieval system, without permission in writing from FriesenPress.

ISBN
978-1-5255-7828-1 (Hardcover)
978-1-5255-7829-8 (Paperback)
978-1-5255-7830-4 (eBook)

1. Poetry, Subjects & Themes, Women Authors

Distributed to the trade by The Ingram Book Company

Contents

Introduction i
Part One: LIVE 1
  Feel 3
  Persona 4
  Youthful Heart 5
  Old Soul 6
  Detour 7
  Silence 8
  Mother 9
  Girls Night 10
  Reflection 11
  Universe 12
  Capulet 13
  Breakup 14
  33 15
  Untitled 16
  Lies 17
  Only Child 18
  Secret 19
  Glad 20
  Dark 21
  Carry 22
Part Two: LOSS 23
  Common 25
  Survival 26

Play Me 27
Pieces 28
New Love 29
His Plan....................... 30
Too Young...................... 31
Fight Club..................... 32
Number 2 33
Ledge.......................... 34
Three Words.................... 35
Walls 36
Fear........................... 37
S&S 38
Mean Girls 39
False 40
The Present 41
Losing You 42
Her............................ 43
Shattered 44

Part Three: LEARN 45
Karma.......................... 47
Degree......................... 48
Fable 49
Fire 50
Traits......................... 51
Blind 52
New Life 53
Evil Twin...................... 54
Attached 55
Simple......................... 56
Écouter 57
Bruises 58
Aim 59

Anxiety 60
Holding on 61
Easy 62
Sweet 63
Cake 64
Husband 65
Rebound 66

Part Four: LOVE **67**
Dream Come True 69
This or that 70
Stop Time 71
Happiness 72
Awake 73
Cliché 74
Constant 75
Fairy Tale 76
1999 77
Us 78
Dirty 79
Hot 80
Fate 81
Feminine 82
Finish 83
Recipe 84
Home 85
Unconditional 86
Fall 87
Belong 88
Full 89
Cognac 90
Sense 91
Spoon 92

This book is dedicated to my
Mom and Papadukes

Introduction

As I packed my bags, in the light of the moon through my bedroom window, I remember replaying the fight over and over in my head, trying to make sense of it all. The house was already devoid of any love, and the loneliness was starting to creep its way in. I grabbed my bags and began walking to the door; I looked back one last time as it seemed like I was leaving my whole life behind. Little did I know my life was just beginning.

This wave of emotion came over me, comprised of anger, relief, sadness, and fear, which led to me breaking down in tears. I cried for the girl who chased lust in her teens and married at 21; I cried for the girl who survived psychological trauma and divorced at 25; and I cried for the woman who was leaving that girl behind once and for all.

What have I learned through it all? Well, all of the pain and heartache that I had lived through as a result of my choices—good and bad—couldn't be for nothing. I needed to make it all mean something. I needed purpose. So I wrote. I wrote so I could heal, and I wrote so I could love again.

I fell in love with words at a very young age, and as an only child, my best friends were books and songs. It is not surprising to me that I became a poet when so much of my life was influenced by these two things, of which, one can argue, are one and the same. My entire life had been leading me to my purpose without me even knowing it.

To me, poetry exists to evoke emotion and touch people through words. This is so we feel less alone, and in that, more understood. I hope you find understanding and peace in this book.

I write to feel lighter but, most importantly, I write for you.

Part One

LIVE

Feel

I am going to let myself go through the emotions
Because that's why God made them

Persona

I am Carrie Bradshaw and
Lorelai Gilmore and
Dorothy Gale and
Snow White and
Katniss Everdeen and
Marilyn Monroe

Youthful Heart

Coffees and vodkas
Nashville and Reggae
Killing me softly
On city nights
Bad highlights and
Dramatic art
Cigarette-smoky skies
Forever a part of
My youthful heart

Old Soul

I am a '40s and '50s girl
In a millennial world

Detour

I usually take the long way around
Alternate routes
Roads less travelled
Chicks had it right

Silence

Sometimes I can't find the words
But the feelings speak to me

Mother

The strongest women I know is made of flesh and bone
She is selfless
And she is fire
She is everything brave and courageous like her sign
She carries burdens for everyone around her
She is often chosen last , by choice
Rarely does she get appreciation and doesn't ask
She is my mother
The strongest women I know
Made of flesh and bone

Girls Night

Martini lights
Dirty cabs
Dog bites
Cheeky grabs

Reflection

Keg talks and
Bar hops
Coffee breaks and
Hand shakes
Busy streets and
Concert beats
Sunday brunches and
Liquid lunches

Universe

You can find me in the stars
Somewhere between heaven and hell
Smiling and laughing with the ones I've lost
And the ones I've loved
Where no judgment lives
Where hatred dies
You better believe
That's where I'll be

Capulet

For you its tractor smoke and northern lights
For me its city smog and taxi nights

Breakup

I may have cried when you left
Turned on the light and wiped away tears
Rising and accumulating fears
Lay there in bed lonely and reaching
Wondering if you were onto the next leaching

33

Forever young
Forever free
Forever in love
Forever me
Forever feeling 33

Untitled

It's not loneliness if you feel free
It is in solitude where I am most creative

Lies

You came and told me what I wanted to hear
You came and cried and apologized
You came and expected what?
You came and explained why
You came and said you changed
You came and wanted me back
You came back
But I was gone

Only Child

I am my fathers daughter
And my mothers best friend
Seeing them in me is how I know
They will always be walking me through life

Secret

You need to find a girl
That is cute and sexy
That's the secret, believe me

Glad

I'm glad you can sleep so well
After leading me to insomnia

Dark

I physically feel ill when we fight
The dark seeps in and removes the light

Carry

The moment I realized I loved you
Was the moment I was afraid to lose you
I believe love co-exists with both emotions
One cannot be without the other
I hope I carry these two through life
With you

Part Two

LOSS

Common

Pain does not discriminate
It does not avoid the strong and latch on to the weak
Fear is similar
Everyone is affected
Sadness inhabits everyone's heart
No one is overlooked
We are all victims
So, you see, we all have something in common

Survival

You take me in your car
You smell like the bar
Telling me you love me
But love isn't what I see
Threatening to drive off the cliff
As you sit and smoke your spliff
Killing us both in your rage
Like I was in a cage
In survival mode
Faking the love you showed
So you would believe me
And I would be able to walk free

Play Me

You're playin' me
I see you cry and you're playin'
I see your text and you're playin' me
Too late for forgiveness
Too late for flirting
Too late for fucking

Pieces

Following my heart
Means letting certain pieces of it go

New Love

The memories are fading and intertwining with the new love
That's how I know I am starting to forget you

His Plan

Remembering can be painful
It's not always a good memory
Not even a fond one
It may even ache
It may bring you to your knees
We try to forget
But His plan is simple
We remember for a reason

Too Young

I remember you flirting with women
As if you weren't married
I remember the gut feeling
As if I knew it was wrong
I remember I was too young to know
As if I had lived already
I remember it being inappropriate
As if I knew what that meant
I would say her name aloud
So people knew you were married
I would yell, "Mom!"
That's how I remember it

Fight Club

I struggle between insecurity and confidence
Some days one overpowers the other and other days
One completely disappears

Number 2

If I washed my life away, oh, it wouldn't be that bad
I could start over and move away the sad
Work my way to being whole again and move away from being with you
I wouldn't cry again or hold grudges like I used to
'Cause your love, it broke me down
And made me feel like I could drown
You awoke demons inside of me
That killed every real part of me
I lost who I was
You had me all to yourself like you wanted it to be
I was alone and you were free
And if I left you, I wouldn't cry or hold grudges like I used to

Ledge

Sometimes I need help walking off the ledge
Accepting the exaggerated conclusion
Help from reaching

Three Words

I miss you
In my head
Your cute laugh
Your brilliant smile
When you walked
Always a hat
And a sweater
In the summer
You would sit
In your chair
Cigarette in hand

Walls

The four walls looked smaller
Your words hit deeper
Prolonged silence and
Misplaced guidance
Panic and anxiety
Afraid of your response
Or responses
Waiting for your words to turn
And your touch to takeover

Fear

Fear hinders my choices
Fear affects my decisions
Fear makes me care what others think
Fear makes me mask my feelings
Fear makes me angry
Fear makes me curl up and cry
Fear makes me hold things in
Fear makes me ashamed
Fear makes me emote every other feeling other than fear

S&S

I can't imagine saying goodbye
I want to have you two all to myself
It's selfish
My heart was full because you were in my life
There will forever be a hole in my heart
Where you two used to be

Mean Girls

I don't want to go
They don't make me feel good
Its like a shadow's cast on my feelings
And my confidence hides
Mean girls are still alive
And remain that way until they're old
It hasn't changed, their auras cold
It still hurts

False

You may have met me under false pretences
And now you don't like what you see
Too bad-this is the real me

The Present

Once upon a time
The world was lost
Waiting to be found
Hiding in pain and fear
She knew love was the only answer
But everyone kept breaking her

Losing You

It feels wrong and it must happen
It's my choice
But I keep asking people for help
Hoping to postpone the inevitable
Losing you

Her

Jealousy kills you from the inside and before you know it
You realize your life is poisoned too

Shattered

I stopped attracting broken people so
I could fix my shattered pieces on my own

Part Three

LEARN

Karma

People are humbled
When things happen to them
That they judged other people for

Degree

I may not measure up to your degree
But I measure up to life experience, kindness and honesty
My extensive library, collected from living and learning
My grades, from my family and friends
I graduate every year of my life
And shine on to the next

Fable

Slow and steady wins the race
I am the tortoise and the heroine in this fable

Fire

Passion and purpose are fuelled by one another
Once the fire is lit
There is no wind nor water
There is not an element strong enough to extinguish it

Traits

I am needy and girly and jealous and fiery and happy and kind and sweet and funny and strong and gracious and humble and vivacious and breathing and feeling and believing and hoping and loving

Blind

I've been so blinded by my hurt that selfishness took over understanding

New Life

My faith in true love is renewed
There is a fire for life that burns inside my soul
This fire had dimmed
Hiding as it was trying to disappear
I think I was trying to disappear
Not from earth
Just from what was around me
The toxicity that was my life
The errors of my past were haunting me
And my past was becoming present again
It wasn't foreign, so I knew what to expect
But it was the same pain
No hiding from that

Evil Twin

Is it really me with the problem
I just can't seem to shake?
The voices—toxic in my head
I just can't seem to erase
All the things that happened
Are still clear in my mind
When I close my eyes, that's all I see
Completely crushing me
I can't explain
I don't know if it will ever go away
I don't know if I need you to go
I don't know what I need
I just want some quiet in my head

Attached

Enabling and manipulation is clear to those who are spectating
But not so clear to those attached by the heart

Simple

Appreciating the simple things
Doesn't make you simple
It makes you gracious

Écouter

There is knowledge in silence
Pay attention to the listeners
They know more than you think

Bruises

Shyness is my curse
I don't wear it lightly
It's heavy and hard
It bruises

Aim

Last night was not fun
Luck wasn't on my side
Anger does not sit right
When it's aimed at you it's unnatural

Anxiety

Nervous about taking the pills that are supposed to be helping me not be nervous

Holding on

Letting go of old friends is like trying to stay young when your old
You just have to embrace that your youth is gone and so are they

Easy

He may see things in you that remind him of his mother, so take it easy on her

Sweet

Falling in love is easy
It's staying in love that's tricky
But when you find the sweet spot
It's priceless

Cake

I don't know what matters most to people but, to me,
The time I share with you I share because I want to, and the quality is the icing on the cake

Husband

I don't want a dream wedding
I want a happy life with a dream husband

Rebound

I used you
To help me forget someone
You were a warm body to curl up to
Someone to distract me and make me feel beautiful again
You were gentle and kind
And you were very useful
You helped me more than you know
And for that I am thankful

Part Four

LOVE

Dream Come True

I always knew he existed
I just thought I would never meet him

This or that

Happiness is a hot summer day on a patio with a pint
And a cool winter frost under a blanket with a chai latte

Stop Time

Because you are my favourite person in the whole world
I never want to be mad at you or have you mad at me
Let's just stay in the place where we are and stop time

Happiness

I am happiest when I am with you
You bring the happy out in me
Happiest when I look at you
Happiest when you smile
Happiest when you hold me
A life full of happiness
Because you are my happy place

Awake

Sometimes I think I am dreaming
Because you can't be real life

Cliché

All the clichés are true—
When you know, you know?
I went to see about a girl
Life is sweeter with you in it
Opposites attract
Love comes to you when you least expect it
Everything happens for a reason
Life brought me to you

Constant

Happiness is the new constant in my life
And the common denominator is you

Fairy Tale

You're my prince charming
My fairy tale
My happily ever after

1999

I love it when you call me
It brings me back to 1999
Faded jeans and love torn scenes

Us

Coffee and tea
That's you and me

Dirty

We wash the linens to get them dirty
We play in the sheets to be shy in the streets

Hot

I woke up so hot for you
My body ached for you
My fountain moistened for you
I was ready for you
And I can feel you ready for me

Fate

My life happened just so, to lead me to you

Feminine

I can be a feminist and still like a man who is chivalrous

Finish

Come over
Come in
Beside me
Inside me
All over me

Recipe

I like you as much as I love you
And that's the recipe for lasting love

Home

Making a house a home with you has become my favourite pastime

Unconditional

I never knew a love like this
So pure
So unconditional
I didn't even want to say goodbye
It would have been too hard
I didn't want you to see me cry
Because you would have felt it, too
I wanted you to live a life so free
So I had to let you go

Fall

She said, "I am scared to fall in love"
He said, "Baby, let's fall together"

Belong

In your arms is where I belong
At least it feels that way when we're close

Full

We don't live in a big place
But it's full of love

Cognac

Cherry lube and dim lighting do the trick
Like needing a cognac with your dick

Sense

This love feels different
It's not an aching, lustful, jealous love
It's a matter-of-fact, partner-in-life, forever love
Because that's the only thing that makes sense

Spoon

You are the perfect snuggle partner
My complementary spoon

CPSIA information can be obtained
at www.ICGtesting.com
Printed in the USA
BVHW030526080221
599332BV00005B/19

9 781525 578298